Dangerous Weather

Written by Paul Shipton

Illustrated by Peter Richardson and Red Giraffe

Hot and sunny

Our planet is called Earth. The Earth travels round the sun. The sun gives us light and heat.

In June it is summer in the north. The weather is hotter and the days are longer.

The sun shines more directly on the middle of the Earth. This is called the Equator.

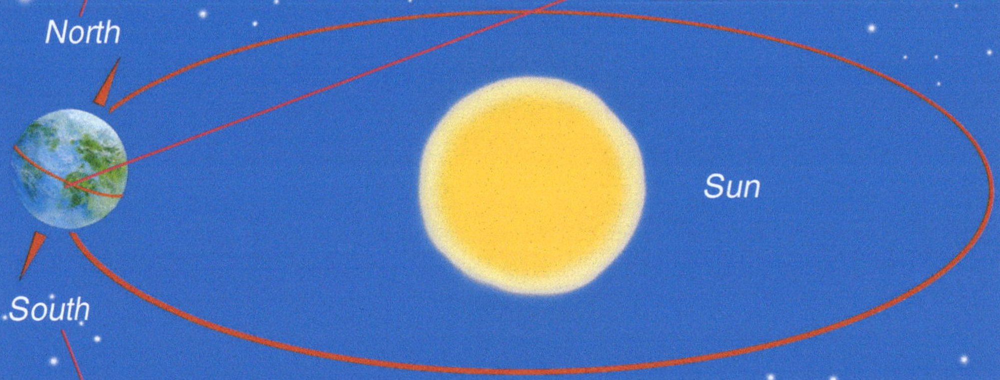

In June it is winter in the south. The weather is colder and the days are shorter.

In a desert there is very little water. But some animals and plants still live there.

This tortoise lives in Death Valley, in the USA. It can get very hot there. Once it was 57° centigrade.

In the Atacama Desert, in Chile, it did not rain for 400 years! In some parts of the desert there are no plants or animals for thousands of miles.

Wet and rainy

Many people in the UK have umbrellas. There are lots of rainy days! But other places in the world are wetter. One mountain in Hawaii can have 350 days of rain a year.

The top of the mountain is cloudy almost all of the time.

Amazing rain

When it is very rainy, in the UK people say, 'It's raining cats and dogs.' But once something similar really happened in the UK. A strong wind picked up some frogs and dropped them in another place!

An area in northern India is very rainy. Once there were nearly twelve metres of rain in one year. It rains from May to October. This is called *Monsoon.* In the winter, there isn't much rain.

When lots of rain falls in a short time there are floods.

Ice and snow

Sometimes cold weather can be very dangerous. A *blizzard* is when it is very snowy and very windy at the same time. It is very hard to see and there are often car accidents.

In 1993 there was a big blizzard in New York, in the USA. There were over 90 centimetres of snow in one day so traffic stopped and the airports closed.

In spring, the snow on mountains melts. Sometimes lots of snow and ice falls down the mountain. This is called an *avalanche*.

An avalanche can cover people, animals and even buildings with snow.

Dogs help people in avalanches. Mountain rescue dogs are big and strong. They can find people in the snow.

Strong winds

Scientists measure the wind.

- A Force 1 or Force 2 wind is very light.
- A Force 6 wind is strong.
- A Force 12 wind is very dangerous. This is called a *hurricane*.

Scientists use satellite photos from space to follow hurricanes. This photo shows a hurricane over the Atlantic Ocean.

A *tornado* is a special wind. It happens in hot weather when the air starts to spin around faster and faster. Tornadoes usually last for about 15 minutes. They can destroy everything in their way. They suck heavy things up into the air – even cars!

The wind in the middle of a tornado can be 400 kilometres an hour.

A tornado destroyed this house.

Thunder and lightning

Sometimes after a hot summer day there is thunder and lightning. Lightning often hits tall buildings and trees.

Did you know that ...

... you can work out how far away a storm is?
Start to count when you see the lightning. Stop when you hear the thunder. For every two seconds, the storm is about one kilometre away.

In 1752, Benjamin Franklin wanted to show that lightning is electricity. He experimented with a kite. He tied a metal key to the kite during a storm. Lightning hit the key and travelled down the kite's wet string.

Benjamin Franklin

! In a storm:
DO NOT stand under a tree.
DO NOT stay in water.
DO NOT walk through a field or up a hill.

Franklin was very lucky! Lightning can kill people. NEVER copy this experiment.

Changing weather

The Earth's weather is changing. Millions of years ago, there were dinosaurs on the Earth. But perhaps the weather killed them. Some people think that a meteor from space hit the Earth 65 million years ago. Clouds of dust stopped the sun's rays. It was too cold for the dinosaurs and they died.

The end of the dinosaurs?

Ten thousand years ago, ice covered 30% of the planet. There were big animals called *mammoths* with woolly coats.

Many people think that humans are changing the Earth's weather. Our pollution is making the weather get hotter.

Air pollution is a big problem in some cities.

Rainforests are very important for the Earth's air. But in the Amazon Rainforest, people cut down trees and burn an area about the size of the UK every year.

You and the weather

People *are* changing the Earth's weather. You can help to stop this.

- Have a shower instead of a bath. It uses less water.
- Don't let the tap run when you brush your teeth.
- Travel by bike or bus instead of the car, to reduce car pollution.
- Recycle your rubbish.

It's easy to recycle.

The Weather Machine

Written by Paul Shipton
Illustrated by Peter Richardson

Katie looked out of the window. It was windy. She wanted to fly her new kite.

Twenty minutes later the children were in a field and Katie's kite was up in the sky. It was fun, but it was VERY windy.

Joel and Katie chased the kite.
Quick! I don't want to lose it! Run!
I AM running!
Run FASTER!

Suddenly the wind stopped. The kite dropped to the ground.
I've got it! That was lucky.
I don't understand. The wind just stopped!

The children looked up. There was a man on the hill. He was next to a big machine. He looked up at the sky and laughed.

Joel wanted to know about the man and his machine.

The man looked up and smiled. There were lots of buttons, lights and wires on the machine.

The Professor pressed a button on the machine and suddenly it was windy again. The weather machine really worked!

The two children listened to Professor Wiggins. He talked about his amazing machine.

The Professor pressed more buttons. Katie and Joel looked up at the blue sky. Suddenly, there were big, dark clouds.

Katie shouted to the Professor over the noise of the heavy rain.

The wind was very strong now. There were leaves and branches in the air. The Professor started to turn off the machine, but he was too slow. Suddenly …

The two children were very scared now. It was very rainy and very windy. They needed to turn off the machine, but there was a big problem. They didn't know how!

Joel pressed a button. Suddenly it started to snow.

Joel pressed more buttons, but the weather did not get better. It was rainy and snowy. The wind was terrible. It was difficult to stand up. Suddenly there was thunder and lightning. Joel pointed at a dark cloud. It moved fast – it was a tornado!

The children were really scared. But then …

... Katie remembered Joel's homework about lightning.
Wait! I've got an idea!
Joel pulled the Professor down the hill. Katie tied a key to the kite. Then she tied the kite to a long wire on the weather machine. She jumped away quickly and watched the kite fly up into the sky.

The tornado was very close to the town now. Suddenly the Professor opened his eyes. They all looked up and watched the kite in the dark sky above them. And then …

... the sky flashed – lightning! It travelled down the wet wire and BOOM! The weather machine exploded!

The tornado disappeared and the wind and rain stopped.
The sky was blue again. The town was safe.

Activities

1 Match the sentences to the pictures.

a Hawaii

b New York

c Northern India

d Atacama Desert

e Amazon Rainforest

1 In 1993, a blizzard stopped all traffic in the city. [b]

2 It did not rain here for 400 years. [ ]

3 People cut down trees and burn an area the size of the UK every year. [ ]

4 There were nearly twelve metres of rain in one year during Monsoon. [ ]

5 It can rain on top of this mountain for 350 days a year. [ ]

2 Write the words.

1 

2 

3 A Force 12 wind is called this.

4 

5 This can happen when there is lots of rain in a short time.

6 

7 This happens when it is very snowy and windy.

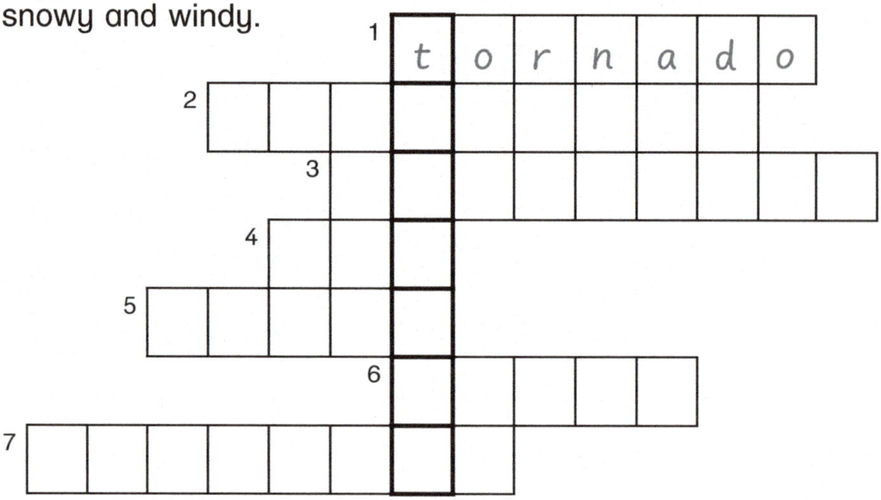

The secret word is ______________________.

3 Circle T (True) or F (False).

1 In summer the days are longer. (T) F

2 Lots of animals live in the Atacama Desert. T F

3 The UK has more rain than any other country. T F

4 In northern India it rains from May to October. T F

5 Tornadoes usually last for about one hour. T F

4 Complete the sentences.

pulled	chased	~~exploded~~	pressed	wanted

1 The weather machine *exploded*.

2 Joel and Katie ______________ the kite.

3 Joel ______________ the Professor down the hill.

4 Joel ______________ a button. Suddenly it started to snow.

5 Katie ______________ to fly her new kite.

5 Find and write the page number from the story.

1 A branch hits Professor Wiggins on the head. [21]

2 Lightning hits the weather machine. [ ]

3 Katie asks Professor Wiggins to turn off the weather machine. [ ]

4 The children fly their kite. [ ]

5 Joel does his homework on the computer. [ ]

6 Katie ties a key to the kite. [ ]

6 Complete the speech bubbles.

raining ~~fly~~ testing dangerous broken

1 Let's go and fly my new kite.

2 Look! It's ____________!

3 I'm sorry, Professor. Your weather machine is ____________.

4 This is my weather machine. I'm ____________ it today.

5 The machine is too ____________.

7 Answer the questions.

1 Is it sunny?

No, it isn't. It's rainy.

2 Is it windy?

____

3 Is it rainy?

____

4 Is it snowy?

____

1

2

3

4

Bilingual Dictionary

Write the words in your language.

air	______________	lose	______________
blizzard	______________	machine	______________
branch	______________	melt	______________
burn	______________	metal	______________
button	______________	meteorite	______________
chase	______________	mountain	______________
cloud	______________	planet	______________
count	______________	pollution	______________
dangerous	______________	ray	______________
desert	______________	recycle	______________
destroy	______________	safe	______________
drop	______________	satellite	______________
dust	______________	shine	______________
electricity	______________	sky	______________
explode	______________	space	______________
fall	______________	spin	______________
field	______________	storm	______________
flash	______________	string	______________
flood	______________	summer	______________
heat	______________	tap	______________
heavy	______________	test	______________
hill	______________	thunder	______________
ice	______________	tie	______________
key	______________	traffic	______________
kite	______________	umbrella	______________
light	______________	winter	______________
lightning	______________	wire	______________

Macmillan Education
4 Crinan Street
London N1 9XW
A division of Springer Nature Limited
Companies and representatives throughout the world

ISBN 978-1-3800-3784-8

First published 2007
This edition published 2019

Illustrated by Peter Richardson and Red Giraffe Limited
Designed by Red Giraffe Limited

The author and publishers would like to thank the following for permission to reproduce their photographs:

Cover Photography with the kind permission of Getty Images/MARS/Cultura RF/Jason Persoff Stormdoctor

Alamy/ John Henry Claude Wilson p5, 27(c), Alamy/ Photo Japan p13(t); Corbis/ Royalty Free p3(t), Corbis/ Douglas Peebles p4, 27(a), Getty Images/ Anna Gorin p7(t); Getty Images/Brand X/Blend Images - REB Images p8(t); Getty Images/Caiaimage/Robert Daly p14(t), Getty Images p1, Getty Images/xeni4ka p3(b), 27(d), Getty Images/Bill Hornstein p6, 27(b), Getty/ Greg Pease p9(l), Getty Images/ Gandee Vasan p10, Getty Images/iStock/Cylonphoto p7(b), Getty Images/Moment/ Willoughby Owen p9(r); PhotoDisc/Getty Images p8(b); Robert Harding World Imagery/ Derrick Furlong p13(b), 27(e); Shutterstock/GUNDAM_Ai p14(b).

Printed and bound in Brazil

2024
6